Australia's
RED HEART
AND TOP END

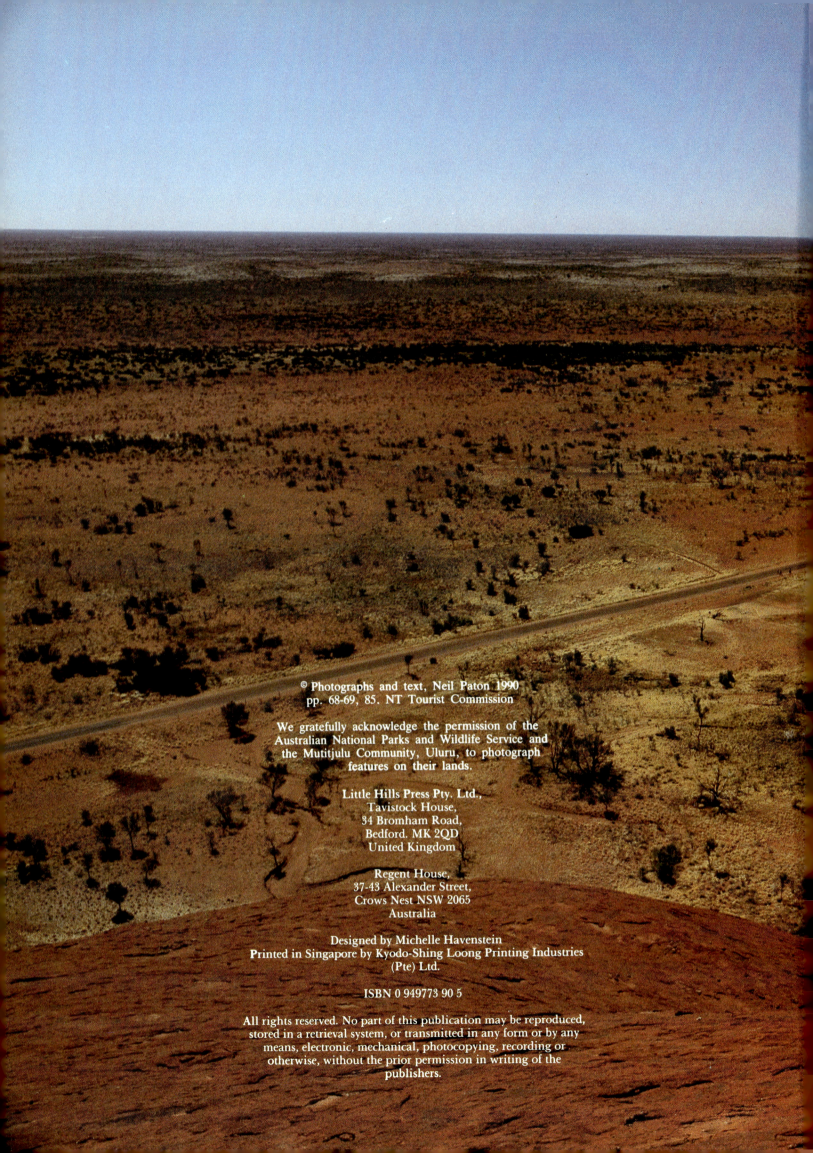

© Photographs and text, Neil Paton 1990
pp. 68-69, 85. NT Tourist Commission

We gratefully acknowledge the permission of the
Australian National Parks and Wildlife Service and
the Mutitjulu Community, Uluru, to photograph
features on their lands.

Little Hills Press Pty. Ltd.,
Tavistock House,
34 Bromham Road,
Bedford. MK 2QD
United Kingdom

Regent House,
37-43 Alexander Street,
Crows Nest NSW 2065
Australia

Designed by Michelle Havenstein
Printed in Singapore by Kyodo-Shing Loong Printing Industries
(Pte) Ltd.

ISBN 0 949773 90 5

All rights reserved. No part of this publication may be reproduced,
stored in a retrieval system, or transmitted in any form or by any
means, electronic, mechanical, photocopying, recording or
otherwise, without the prior permission in writing of the
publishers.

Australia's RED HEART AND TOP END

NEIL PATON

CONTENTS

INTRODUCTION 6

RED HEART
ALICE SPRINGS 11

AYERS ROCK 19
The Olgas, Mt Connor, Kings Canyon

MACDONNELL RANGES 39
Ormiston Gorge, Glen Helen Gorge, Arltunga, Ross River,
N'Dhala Gorge

CHAMBERS PILLAR & RAINBOW VALLEY 63
Ewaninga

TOP END
DARWIN 71

KAKADU NATIONAL PARK 77
Katherine Gorge National Park

MAP 87

INDEX 88

Left Kantju Gorge, Ayers Rock.

INTRODUCTION

Where a huge inland sea was once situated, a desert is now found. The desert was first peopled by the Aborigines, who arrived in Australia perhaps 50,000 years ago. They are thought to have arrived in the Centre at least 10,000 years ago. During this time, they have kept their culture alive and it has left its mark in the form of innumerable paintings, rock carvings and grinding grooves, many of which can still be seen at Ayers Rock (Uluru), N'Dhala Gorge, Ewaninga and Trephina Gorge among other places.

Just as Australia could not remain insulated from the rest of the world forever, so the Centre could not remain insulated from the rest of the Colony. By the 1850s European explorers were probing northwards in their attempts to solve the mystery of what lay at the heart of the Great South Land. The first to finally reach the Centre and Top End was a diminutive Scotsman named John McDouall Stuart, who must rank as one of the greatest, most stubborn, pig-headed and determined explorers this country has known. After some earlier travels in the 1850s in company with other explorers, Stuart led expeditions in 1858 and 1859, finally reaching the geographical centre of Australia on April 22, 1860. His eyesight and health suffered from the journeys but he returned to cross the continent from south to north in 1862. Carried back on a litter because of ill health, he was lionised on his return to Adelaide. He died five years later after returning to his native Scotland.

The pivotal development in the ensuing years was the construction of the Overland Telegraph Line, from south to north, following largely in Stuart's footsteps. A telegraph station was established in the Centre, adjacent to a waterhole on the usually dry Todd River. The waterhole became known as Alice Springs, and on the south side of the telegraph station a town eventually developed which was known originally as Stuart, in honour of John McDouall. Stuart became the focal point of the Centre and the deserts became the home of cattle that grazed on thinly vegetated properties. The diverse features of the area—from Ayers Rock to Chambers Pillar, the MacDonnell Ranges, Mt Sonder and many more—became known, mapped and familiar. Clashes between Aboriginals and European settlers inevitably took place and resulted in a substantial reduction of the Aboriginal population. The Aranda people were considered to be in danger of extinction at one stage and this led to the establishment of places like the

Above Aboriginal paintings at Nourlangie Rock.
Right Tourists returning after completing the popular but demanding climb of Ayers Rock.

Hermannsburg Mission, where Aboriginals were housed to ensure their survival. Such well-intentioned acts often showed little understanding of, or respect for, the Aboriginal culture, and generally Aboriginals did not live on their own terms. Thus, they survived but were reduced to the role of dependents living on handouts.

Western society, meanwhile, developed an increasing interest in the Centre and the Top End as that twentieth century growth industry, tourism, began to boom. Today the Northern Territory is firmly on the itinerary of tourists from Australia and overseas. Yulara Resort, built especially to handle the traffic, accommodates a floating and cosmopolitan population of 5,000 people. Alice Springs has grown rapidly and Darwin, re-built after being destroyed by Cyclone Tracey, is emerging as a major centre. Nowadays, the Territory is accessible to anyone who can afford the fare. We can all follow in Stuart's footsteps without ruining our health or eyesight. The Red Centre and Top End belong to everyone.

RED HEART

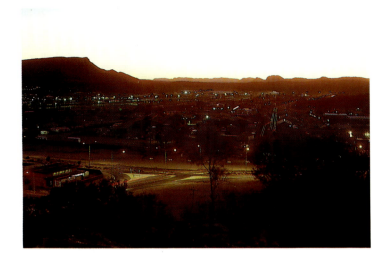

ALICE SPRINGS

The Alice came into being entirely because of the Colony's desire for increased and improved contact with the outside world. Both internal and external connections were sluggish, internal depending on morse code and external on slow-moving ships. A telegraph line linking the south with the north, and joining a newly established submarine cable in the north, would considerably improve communication. Sir Charles Todd, the Superintendent of Telegraphs in South Australia, fought hard to have the telegraph line built from Adelaide to the newly founded Port Darwin in the north. Todd had his way and the mammoth task of building the overland line was completed by 1872. It was not completed without loss of life, as is borne out by a grave that can still be seen north of Alice, outside Wigley Gorge, bearing a plaque with the inscription:

IN MEMORY
OF
C.PALMER
TEAMSTER O.T.LINE
DIED 1870

The Telegraph Station was established near the Todd River, and a town was surveyed by David Lindsay, the Government Surveyor, in 1888. Geographically, the most distinctive feature of the area was its site in the middle of the MacDonnell Ranges and adjacent to the Todd River. The MacDonnell Ranges were described by Stuart as the first real mountain range he had seen since leaving the Flinders, and they give Alice Springs an ambience quite different from that of the flat hinterland beyond. The Todd River begins some kilometres north of Alice Springs and meanders south, joining the Finke River until it fizzles out further south in the desert. Both rivers are usually dry apart from occasional waterholes like the one that became known as Alice Springs. They flow only after heavy rain—usually in summer—and sometimes cause significant flooding, but like most outback rivers they rarely flow along their entire length.

The town of Alice Springs, or Stuart as it was then known, was established on the flat land immediately west of the Todd River and south of the Telegraph Station, and grew as the administrative and commercial heart of Central Australia. It was joined by rail to Adelaide when the old Ghan line was built in 1929, an event of considerable excitement and significance for the

Previous pages Rainbow Valley.
Above Alice Springs at dusk, seen from Anzac Hill.
Left The busy town centre of Alice Springs.

people of Stuart. The line never reached Darwin, as was originally planned. With the development of the railway line the town's name was changed to Alice Springs in 1933.

A key event in the development of the town was the arrival of the Reverend John Flynn, who rode through the MacDonnell Ranges on a camel and, it is said, found himself overwhelmed by a sense of belonging. Flynn, born in 1880, founded the Australian Inland Mission and the Flying Doctor Service; he also spurred Alfred Traeger to develop the pedal radio, which became of crucial importance in the Centre. Flynn was also responsible for the establishment and design of Adelaide House, the first hospital in Central Australia. The hospital was built on the recommendation of Sister Finlayson, who worked for the Australian Inland Mission. Flynn designed the house in such a way that it would be cool and comfortable in the hot summer months, with a central hall rising above the roof to promote ventilation, wide verandahs to provide shade and an "air conditioning system" that consisted of a deep cellar and air ducts leading to all sections of the building. The house became a museum in 1980 and has since undergone restoration; it now stands as one of the few historical buildings to have survived the modern development of Alice Springs.

Flynn was also instrumental in establishing the Old Timers' Home on the Stuart Highway. With his close associate, Kingsley Partridge, Flynn saw the need for a comfortable home where old people around the Centre could retire and be cared for. As with Adelaide House, the versatile Flynn was again the designer, and the Old Timers' Home opened in 1949.

Flynn died at Royal Prince Alfred Hospital, Sydney, in 1951. The internment of his ashes took place outside Alice Springs on May 23, 1951; the town closed down for the day and the whole of the outback listened in on the radio. The ashes, encased in a steel box, were placed in a cairn at the foot of Mt Gillen, one of Flynn's favourite places and the spot where he had said he would like to be buried. The ashes of Flynn's wife, Joan, were added to the cairn in 1969. Flynn was one of those people who lived to see all his dreams come true, and he changed the Centre in the process.

Today, Alice Springs has a population of well over 20,000 and is one of the most rapidly growing towns in the country. As the commercial heart of the Centre, it has naturally felt the effects of the increased tourist traffic that has developed over the years, with the mixed results that tourism brings. Along with more jobs and more money, tourism inevitably brings a certain gloss which can be either prosperous or plastic, depending on who it affects. People who have known Alice for several years sometimes complain that the town is getting too "touristy", and undeniably it has a certain brashness. Little of its early architecture has survived, and the "face" presented by the town is largely one of concrete and glass. Nevertheless, Alice is growing while many provincial towns are dying, and that alone is an achievement in the harsh land we know as the Centre.

Left Aboriginals preparing for a Corroboree.
Right, above Adelaide House, the first hospital in Central Australia.
Right, below The Alice Springs, the waterhole from which the town eventually took its name.
Following pages The rugged shapes of the Heavitree Range, looking west from Mt Gillen.

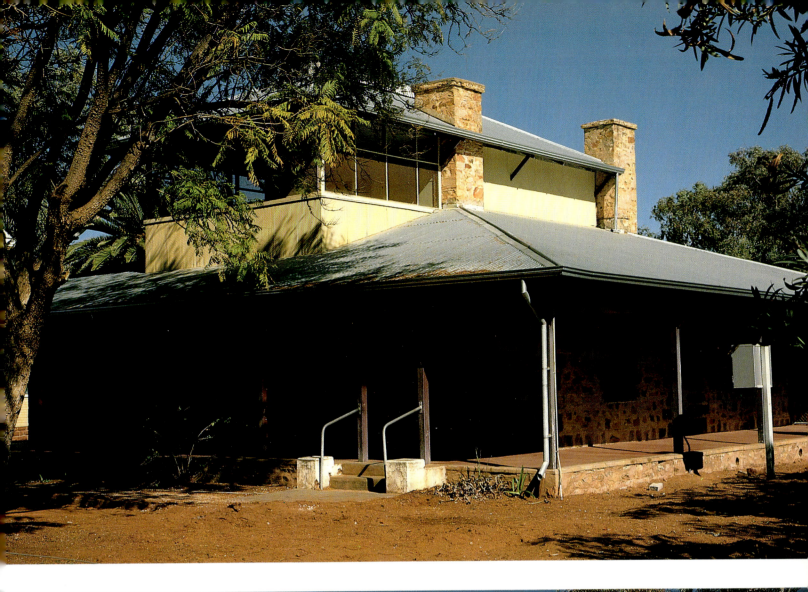

Above left A view of Alice from the Heavitree Range.
Below left Mt Gillen. **Top** Coach rides are popular in Alice Springs. **Above** The Old Telegraph Station, around which the town of Alice Springs originally developed.

AYERS ROCK
The Olgas, Mt Conner, Kings Canyon

Most of the features of the Centre, including the famous Ayers Rock, are broadly west or south-west of Alice Springs. The western part of the Centre is heavily travelled and endowed with natural features in a series of national parks and reserves. The Mecca is, of course, Ayers Rock (Uluru), where buses and cars pull up every day and cameras are clicked by the hundred. Many visitors are content to simply gaze at the Rock, and perhaps see it glow a fiery orange at sunset. For some it is an achievement to climb the Rock as far as the beginning of the chain that goes up the steepest section. Others climb all the way to the summit, leaving their names in the visitors' book. Relatively few walk along the top of the Rock traversing the steep corrugations to see the little-known pools, trees and shrubs.

Ayers Rock is part of a group of three formations collectively known as the Three Great Tors. The other two are the Olgas (Katatjuta) and Mt Conner; they are in a straight line that stretches for just over 120 kilometres. Mt Conner and the Rock are composed of sandstone while the Olgas are of conglomerate rock; all three stand above the surrounding desert resisting the effects of erosion. The Olgas, in contrast to the jutting shape of Ayers Rock, consist of a group of more than thirty domes, the largest of which is Mt Olga. From a distance, the Olgas look remarkably like the set from a science fiction film, while to walk among them is to feel like one is in a lunar landscape. Ayers Rock is famous for its changes of colour. The Olgas probably present even more of a spectrum. Before sunrise they glow with opalescent blues and mauves; during the day they are as orange as the Rock at close quarters but tinged with a pastel mauve when seen from a distance; after sunset they turn blue and purple. A little known fact is that the Olgas have a number of gum trees that create the same bluish tinge that is seen so vividly in the Blue Mountains of New South Wales. The Olgas are a favourite with tourists.

The third member of the group, Mt Conner, has been described as the "forgotten residual of Central Australia". A sprawling sandstone mesa, Mt Conner is situated approximately 90 kilometres east of Ayers Rock. Although it does not possess the dominating presence of the Rock, Mt Conner is

Left Kantju Gorge, Ayers Rock. **Above** The characteristically hulking shapes of Ayers Rock.

as striking and beautiful in its own way. Roughly horseshoe-shaped, it can be climbed on the south side but is not easily reached. Unlike Ayers Rock and the Olgas, Mt Conner is part of the Curtin Springs property. Permission can be obtained to visit the mountain, but the tracks that lead to it are suitable only for four-wheel drive vehicles.

The Curtin Springs property is also the site of another little known feature of the Centre: the grave of a young pioneer traveller named Ellis Bankin. Bankin was a schoolteacher who had travelled around Australia a great deal on his motorbike, and during a trip to Alice Springs he developed an interest in the areas further to the west. In those days—the 1930s—it was necessary to obtain permission to visit Ayers Rock and there were no roads into the area, merely camel tracks. Bankin obtained the necessary permit and set off on his bike in December, 1935, intending an extensive tour. He visited a number of outback stations on his way to Ayers Rock. Eventually reported missing, he perished, and was found somewhere near Mt Conner. It will never be known whether he headed for Mt Conner deliberately, or mistook it for Ayers Rock. Today he is largely forgotten, but perhaps deserves a humble place in the history of the Centre, as a kind of pioneering traveller who took on the Centre at a time when few people were interested in it.

North of Mt Conner is the long, serrated escarpment of the George Gill Range, which includes Kings Canyon, rapidly becoming one of the better known features of the Centre. The canyon has spectacular cliff formations as well as the contrasting worlds of the Lost City and the Garden of Eden. The former consists of an array of bee-hive shaped rock formations along the north rim of the canyon; they tend to be reminiscent of the Bungle Bungle Range in Western Australia, although on a smaller scale. To walk between them is to see how appropriately they have been named, for it does not require much imagination to see the bee-hive shapes as a kind of ancient biblical city.

At the east end of the canyon, a long twisting gully gives rise to another world known as the Garden of Eden. Trees adorn long, rocky pools, creating a shady sanctuary that provides a perfect contrast to the bare rocks of the Lost City, as well as welcome relief on a hot day. A rough foot-track leads through the Garden of Eden to a sheer drop from which a spectacular view of the canyon can be obtained. After heavy rain, this spot becomes the site of a waterfall that drops down to Kings Creek, the principal watercourse of the canyon. Another rough track provides a walk along the floor of the canyon, but only an abseiler could get from the Garden of Eden to the floor below.

Above The sunrise view of Ayers Rock, to which visitors flock every day.

Above Ayers Rock (Uluru as it is called by the Aboriginal people) seen from a different perspective.
Left Imalung Lookout at Yulara provides the tourist with this view of 'The Rock'.
Below left Sunset at Ayers Rock heralds a flock of tourists to sight the change of colour.
Following pages Aboriginal art has attracted the attention of many, and gives an insight into the culture of the various tribes.

Above A fig tree growing on the lower slopes of Ayers Rock. **Above right** Rock shelters like this are a common sight as one walks around Ayers Rock. **Below right** The Olgas, seen here after sunset, provide a beautiful backdrop for Yulara. **Following pages** An overall view of the Olgas.

Top left The Valley of the Winds, the site of one of the walking tracks through the Olgas.

Left Wild flowers in the Red Heart give a colourful result of recent rains.

Top An example of the broken and scattered formations that make the Olgas look so different from Ayers Rock.

Above The red earth of The Centre provides a contrasting colour to the delicate mauves of flowers from a hardy bush after rains.

Following pages Mt Conner turning a vivid pink at sunset.

Above left Sand dunes on the Curtin Springs property, typical of the Central Australian terrain. **Below left** An electrical storm at Curtin Springs. **Above** The spectacular view of Kings Canyon from above the waterfall.
Following pages The jagged cliffs flanking Ellery Creek, Northern Territory.

Top The Lost City, a strange world of bee-hive rock formations along the north rim of Kings Canyon. **Above** Another view of the distinctive formations in the Lost City. **Right** The Garden of Eden, an idyllic, winding gully that feeds the waterfall of Kings Canyon in the Wet season.

MACDONNELL RANGES

North-east of the George Gill Range is the spreadeagled shape of the MacDonnell Ranges. John McDouall Stuart had compared the MacDonnells to the Flinders Ranges in South Australia, and the comparison is by no means fanciful, since the ranges present similarly spectacular shapes and forms. To stand on some peaks in the MacDonnells is to look at a text-book illustration of how mountain ranges can be formed, with the gradual southern slopes and the broken northern surfaces giving eloquent testimony to how the land was pushed up at an angle, creating smooth slopes on one side and crumbling cliffs on the other. Formed during the Devonian Period and composed mainly of quartz, the MacDonnells stretch for four hundred kilometres and are now the home of a number of national parks and reserves. Many of the features that draw travellers today consist of spectacular gaps in the ranges, frequently blocked by permanent waterholes. The ranges have also created a number of gorges—like Redbank Gorge, Ormiston Gorge and Glen Helen Gorge—which provide some of the most dramatic scenery in Central Australia as well as opportunities for a number of interesting walks. While the MacDonnells are not as well known as Ayers Rock and never will be, they provide the visitor with the opportunity to feast on mountain scenery that some people consider one of the best features of the Centre. It is not hard to see why John Flynn, standing on the peak of Mt Gillen, felt so in love with the mountains and why it was the place where he wanted to be buried.

Further east of Alice Springs, the MacDonnells continue their jagged course to the vicinity of Arltunga, where they are at their widest with a breadth of 120 kilometres. The scenery of the East MacDonnells is less well known and probably less visited than that of the West MacDonnells; most Australians have probably seen photos of Standley Chasm and are at least vaguely familiar with the images of the West MacDonnells depicted in the paintings of Albert Namatjira, but few of us are familiar with Emily Gap, Jessie Gap or Corroboree Rock. Emily Gap is the first of the gaps to the east of Alice Springs and is blocked by a permanent

Left The spectacular Ormiston Gorge. **Above** N'Dhala Gorge, site of thousands of Aboriginal rock carvings.

waterhole. On the east side of the gap there are some elaborate Aboriginal paintings, but the waterhole makes access difficult. On the south side of the gap can be found a good species of a shield tree, where an oval gap was left in the bark after the Aboriginals had cut a shield out of it.

Jessie Gap lies further east and is one of the few gaps that can be walked through, since it is not blocked by water. Only after heavy rain, most likely around January or February, would Jessie Gap be the site of a waterhole of any pretensions. Both Jessie and Emily Gaps are contained within a national park, and are popular recreation spots, particularly when summer temperatures make the waterhole at Emily Gap an irresistible temptation. Visitors are sometimes delighted to see brumbies (wild horses) drinking water on the northern edge of the waterhole.

Thirty kilometres east of Jessie Gap lies Corroboree Rock, the centrepiece of a conservation reserve. The rock was of great religious significance to the Aranda people who inhabited this part of the Centre. Sacred objects were stored at the rock and young men were taken there to be instructed by tribal elders. The name Corroboree Rock, however, is something of a misnomer, since it is generally accepted that corroborees—religious dances—did not take place there.

An array of nature reserves is encountered further east, beginning with Trephina Gorge Nature Park, situated on Trephina Creek. The gorge is the site of a number of walking tracks and provides the opportunity for enough walks to make it worth spending a few days in the area. Camping is allowed, and the observant will notice Aboriginal paintings on the rocky walls of the gorge. Another feature of the area is John Hayes Rockhole, which can be reached by a walking track from the gorge and which is named after a member of the family that has run the Undoolya Station, north of Jessie Gap, for many years.

Trephina Creek leads to Ross River, the site of a large property which has been turned into a tourist resort. The Ross River Homestead goes back to 1876, when a grazing lease was taken up in the area. The property changed hands a couple of times and was owned at one stage by Louis Bloomfield, who bred horses for the British Army in India. The

Bloomfields are still neighbours at Ross River and have given their name to Bloomfields Bluff, an imposing cliff-face overlooking a stretch of the Ross River. As a resort, the homestead now provides accommodation in cabins and at a rudimentary campground, while also providing camel safaris and boomerang-throwing lessons, plus demonstrations in making damper and boiling the billy. The atmosphere is casual and the property still retains an outback character, while the beautiful valley in which it is situated provides plenty of opportunity for photographers and walkers.

Ten kilometres south of Ross River Homestead lies N'Dhala Gorge Nature Park, the site of literally thousands of Aboriginal rock carvings that are thought to be among the oldest known carvings in Australia. An unsealed road leads to the beginning of the gorge, where a small clearing makes camping possible. From the clearing, a walking track winds along the gorge's rocky floor, making it possible to view carvings as one walks along. The carvings are by no means conspicuous but the careful observer will always find something of interest. Anyone familiar with the grooved rock carvings of other areas will notice the contrast with the "pecked" carvings of N'Dhala Gorge.

At the furthest and widest end of the East MacDonnells is a 5,000 hectare area known as Arltunga Historical Reserve. Arltunga is an abandoned gold-mining town where gold was found in 1887. Originally, the finds were alluvial gold in creek beds, but the quartz reefs yielded a rich store of gold some years later. Today, these quartz reefs still protrude conspicuously from the ground and the mines can be inspected by visitors. Arltunga was a larger town than Alice Springs for some time before going into decline. The ruins— including two cemeteries, the police station, gaol, official quarters and cyanide works—were taken over by the Northern Territory Reserves Board in 1975 and restoration work has been carried out on the buildings. Arltunga is now considered one of the most significant historic goldfields in the country. In the western part of the reserve there is a tourist park with campground, camel farm and corrugated-iron bush pub to provide refreshments. Further east of Arltunga, a four-wheel drive road leads to Ruby Gorge Nature Park, a rugged area that is not heavily frequented but whose very isolation is an attraction in itself, making it possible to experience that feeling of being completely away from civilisation. Camping is permitted.

Left A lizard, in this case a goanna, shows that life can exist in the Red Heart.
Above Historic buildings at the Arltunga Reserve have been preserved in a large heritage site in the East MacDonnell Ranges.

Top Glen Helen Gorge, one of the major attractions of the West MacDonnells. **Above** A view of Ormiston Gorge from the main walking track in the area. **Right** Palm Valley, renowned for its rare cabbage palms.

Above left Further downstream of Palm Valley is Cycad Gorge, named after the cycad palms found along its slopes.
Below left Mt Sonder, regarded by many as the most beautiful peak in the MacDonnells.

Above A kangaroo surprised by the photographer.
Top The old Church, Hermannsburg Mission.
Following pages Afternoon light in the East MacDonnells.

Above left Jagged shapes of the East MacDonnells.
Below left Emus are one of the animal species that inhabit the Red Heart in large numbers.
Above Aboriginal paintings near the waterhole at Emily Gap.

Left A ghost gum, a familiar sight in the MacDonnell Ranges. **Top** Jessie Gap, one of the few gaps in the MacDonnells that can be walked through because it is not blocked by a waterhole. **Above** Corroboree Rock, once the site of Aboriginal initiation ceremonies. **Following pages** Trephina Gorge, centre-piece of one of the national parks found in the East MacDonnells.

Left A bush of wild flowers changes the face of Australia's Red Heart after rain.
Top An overall view of Bloomfields Bluff.
Above A late afternoon scene at the Ross River Homestead.

Above left The sun goes down at Ross River Homestead.
Below left Outback paraphernalia at Ross River. **Above and following pages** General views of N'Dhala Gorge.

Below left A gold mine at Arltunga. Ladders make the mine accessible to visitors. **Above left and above** Historic remnants from the gold-mining days, Arltunga. **Top** One of many stone buildings preserved and restored at Arltunga.

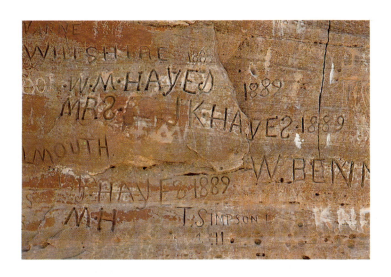

CHAMBERS PILLAR AND RAINBOW VALLEY

South of Alice Springs, the MacDonnells give way to more of the sprawling, semi-arid desert that is the essence of the Centre. Cattle still graze on properties like the Maryvale Station, a hundred kilometres south of Alice, but the nearby ruins of the "Bokhara" homestead remind us that the country is not always hospitable. The Aboriginals survived there by knowing their water supplies, and the Ewaninga Conservation Reserve provides an example of the mark they left behind. A claypan provided a supply of water that might have lasted for some months after heavy rain, and this meant that the area was used constantly by Aboriginals until they would eventually be forced to move on to the waterholes of the MacDonnells. Adjacent to the claypan, a number of rocks are adorned with hundreds of pecked carvings, or "petroglyphs". Details like birds' feet can still deciphered, in spite of some of the rocks having obviously broken up and crumbled. A large number of axe-grinding grooves can also be seen. Needless to say, all Aboriginal sites are protected.

One hundred and sixty kilometres south of Alice Springs is the best known feature of this part of the Centre, Chambers Pillar. The Pillar is an example of a sandstone mesa that has been eroded to the point where only a column is left standing. The first European to see this fifty metre high landmark was John McDouall Stuart, who reached Chambers Pillar in 1860. He named it after James Chambers, an Adelaide businessman who was one of the sponsors of Stuart's expedition. The Pillar was also visited in 1870 by John Ross and in 1872 by the explorer Ernest Giles. Gradually, more people began to see the Pillar and to leave their names carved into the sandstone surface. Names that can clearly be seen include that of John Hayes, and dates from the late nineteenth century can still be made out. Unfortunately, latter-day explorers disguised as tourists have been inspired to emulate their predecessors and the Pillar is now thoroughly ringed with names and initials. Presumably, visitors will one day carve right through the Pillar.

Chambers Pillar is the focal point of a group of rock formations, including one called Castle Rock. In Aboriginal mythology, Chambers Pillar

Left Desert oaks frame a rock formation near Chambers Pillar. **Above** Historic carvings at Chambers Pillar. They have unfortunately been joined by carvings of a less historic nature.

Following pages The dramatic shapes and colours of Rainbow Valley.

was originally the Gekko ancestor Itirkawara, who violated the marriage code by marrying a girl from the wrong kin group. He and his wife were banished to the desert, where Itirkawara turned into Chambers Pillar, and his wife, stricken with shame, turned into Castle Rock. Chambers Pillar and the formations around it create a place of enormous atmosphere and character, an ideal spot to spend a night in the desert. The whole area south of Alice Springs is notable for the bizarre formations of which Chambers Pillar and its companions are only a part. Groups of mesas are seen side-by-side with long, sprawling ridges and pyramid-shaped hills, creating a strange landscape.

Between Chambers Pillar and Alice Springs lies a little known place that is now a proposed nature reserve. Rainbow Valley is a startlingly unique system of sandstone ridges on the edge of a broad claypan. Time and the elements have broken the sandstone up into jagged outcrops streaked with surprisingly rich bands of orange and brown. The main ridge has broken up into saw-toothed shapes that sometimes provoke visitors to observe that "it looks like someone took a bite out of it". On the south side, the sand dunes allow laborious access to the top of the ridge and views of the surrounding area. A public outcry put a stop to plans to mine the area for sandstone, and Rainbow Valley now takes a unique place in the system of parks in Central Australia.

Above Ruins of Bokhara, a failed sheep station near the Maryvale property. **Above right** Chambers Pillar, the remains of a sandstone mesa. **Below right** Castle Rock, one of the distinctive formations that give the Chambers Pillar area much of its character.

TOP END

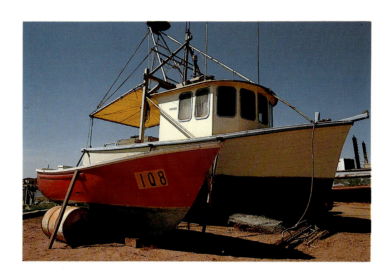

DARWIN

The Northern Territory comprises about a sixth of the total area of Australia, with Darwin as its capital. The city has a population of about 70,000, making it the smallest capital in Australia but one of the most individualistic. Having gone through a number of changes and transformations over the years, Darwin has emerged as a thriving capital strategically placed on the doorstep of Asia.

Darwin's origins go back to the 1820s, when the Territory was incorporated in New South Wales and unsuccessful attempts were made to develop settlements near the present site. The intrepid John McDouall Stuart reached the northern coast in 1862 and in the following year control of the Territory was handed over to South Australia. What was then known as Palmerston was selected for development in 1869 and in 1870 the Overland Telegraph Line was begun. With the line successfully constructed, the first telegraph communication between Australia and England was made in 1871.

Developments proceeded rapidly with the discovery of gold at Pine Creek in 1872. Darwin's cosmopolitan character partly goes back to the goldrush days, which brought an influx of miners from other countries. Many of them were Chinese and their most visible legacy is the Taoist Temple in Woods Street. It is still used for worship as well as being a popular tourist attraction.

A proposed Adelaide-Darwin railway line began in 1877 but obviously did not move very quickly, since it did not crawl into Alice Springs until 1929. Further extension of the line from Alice Springs to Darwin has foundered on the controversial question of whether the line would ever by viable. Even without the railway line, however, settlement of the north proceeded apace with the discovery of copper in 1882 at Daly River and pearl shells offshore from Darwin. Huge cattle properties also commenced operation, particularly on the Barkly Tablelands, and the development of the Top End was well underway.

In the early decades of the 20th Century, Darwin was still an easy-going tropical town, but the Second World War shook the residents, and spurred more development. Interstate communications were improved and the population expanded, while Japanese air-raids were a reminder that even sleepy Australia could not insulate itself from the rest of the world forever. Further construction of the city was rapid, but no-one foresaw that an enormous setback lay ahead.

On Christmas Eve, 1974, Cyclone Tracy entered

Previous pages Unchallenged king of the Top End, the crocodile should be treated with a lot of respect.

Left The Performing Arts Centre, Darwin. **Above** Fishing boats at Frances Bay.

the history books when it rampaged through Darwin and virtually wiped out the city. The rest of the country responded immediately as the news of Darwin's devasation came through. Charity agencies worked around the clock to take in donations and send them to Darwin. The city was virtually evacuated while building commenced, and before long a new city emerged, Phoenix-like, and relegated Cyclone Tracy to the status of an unpleasant memory. The episode was etched into the psyche of the nation, so that Cyclone Tracy has become a by-word for carnage and destruction, and has even been immortalised in a popular song, "Santa Never Made It Into Darwin".

In the 1980s, however, Darwin has become one of the most modern cities in the world as well as one of the most cosmopolitan. Visitors enjoy its free-and-easy atmosphere, dictated partly by the tropical climate which makes casual clothing a necessity. In the Dry season, especially, Darwin becomes a tourist mecca, with visitors being drawn by the thousands to the area's natural beauties and outdoor recreations. A glance at a map shows how Darwin is located strategically between the main cities of Australia and South-East Asia, and it is destined to become more important as the countries of the Pacific Rim develop economically. Furthermore, it is the gateway to Australia's two most famous national parks, Uluru and Kakadu, and this fact alone ensures the importance of Darwin as a stop-off point for the world's travellers.

It is not only Uluru and Kakadu, however, that are of interest. Around the city can be found a number of historic buildings as well as places and events of general interest. An historic walk around Darwin could take in Lyons Cottage, Government House, the former Admiralty House, the old Police Station and Court House, Christ Church Cathedral, Browns Mart Theatre, the Old Town Hall, the Victoria Hotel and the Chinese Temple. More unusual attractions can be found at Doctors Gully and the Crocodile Farm. At the former, visitors flock to the water's edge to feed the fish every day at high tide. This ritual began casually when bread was thrown to some fish and they kept coming back for more; it is now a regular feature of life in Darwin. At the Crocodile Farm off the Stuart Highway, visitors can see how over 7,000 crocodiles are bred commercially for their skins, and can watch them being fed.

Further afield, a network of nature parks and reserves provides an outstanding range of outdoor attractions and activities. Casuarina Coastal Reserve, on the north side of Darwin, features pockets of monsoon forest and World War Two gun emplacements situated alongside a beach and

picnic area. Nude bathing is allowed in the declared "free beach" area. Holmes Jungle Nature Park, at the north-east end of Darwin, contains areas of wet monsoon forest. Picnic facilities are provided and elevated walkways make it possible to explore parts of the forest.

Howard Springs Nature Park consists of over a thousand hectares of nature area centred on a large, spring-fed pool. Visitors can swim in the pool all year round as well as make use of the walking tracks. Fish and other wildlife are plentiful, while ducks and geese can be hunted in the Hunting Reserve during the declared season.

Berry Springs Nature Park also features spring-fed pools in its 247 hectares. Wet monsoon forest can be seen along Berrys Creek and an open-range nature park is being developed on adjacent land by the Conservation Commission. Closer to Darwin, the Yarrawonga Zoo houses a wide-ranging collection of native animals as well as introduced species.

Fogg Dam Conservation Reserve, east of Darwin along the Arnhem Highway, consists of 1,569 hectares of permanent wetlands which attract a large number of waterbirds. Visitors can observe a range of birds that includes egrets, Australian ibises, herons, brolgas, ducks and pied geese. Leaning Tree Lagoon Nature Park, also reached via the Arnhem Highway, protects a large lagoon that serves as a refuge for waterbirds in the Dry season. Visitors to the 101 hectare reserve are also attracted by the opportunity for water sports.

The Mary River Crossing Reserve is an area of over 2,500 hectares and includes permanent lagoons that, like Leaning Tree Lagoon, serve as a refuge for waterbirds in the Dry season. The Mary River is well-known for its barramundi fishing, and a variety of wildlife, including different species of wallaby, can be found among the granite formations of the area. Bordering the Mary River network, the Wildman River Reserve is a refuge of over 24,000 heectares. With its permanent billabongs, as well as the river, it is popular for boating and fishing.

Litchfield Park is one of the best-kept secrets of the Top End. Close to the town of Bachelor, south of Darwin, it comprises 65,000 hectares of land with waterfalls, hot springs and rainforests. Among its features are the giant magnetic termite mounds which frequently tower over visitors. For those with four-wheel drive, the Tabletop Range also offers outstanding scenic attractions.

Left Sunset at Mindil Beach. Above Government House

Above left Twilight falls on fishing boats at Frances Bay.
Below left Nightcliff Beach, a popular swimming spot on the north side of Darwin. **Top** Darwin's Chinese Temple, one of the few authentic Taoist temples in Australia. **Above** The Smith Street Pedestrian Mall, the heart of Darwin.

KAKADU NATIONAL PARK
Katherine Gorge National Park

In recent years, Kakadu has become the most famous national park in Australia as well as our best-known World Heritage area. An area of 19,000 square kilometres has been preserved within the park, based primarily on the Alligator River systems that flow from Arnhem Land to Van Diemen Gulf. Within this area, a broad range of landscapes is found, from the stony ground of the Arnhem Land Escarpment to sprawling woodland, wetlands, rivers and billabongs. An enormous range of wildlife finds refuge in the park, many of which are rare and even unique to Kakadu. Over 1,000 types of plants have been identified, plus 55 kinds of fish, 25 kinds of frogs, 75 reptiles, 275 species of birds and 50 mammal species.

Kakadu is not, however, significant only for its scenery and wildlife. Australian Aboriginals have lived in the area for at least 25,000 years, and some think it is possible that they could have been there since their arrival on the continent some 50,000 years ago. They established an artistic tradition that still survives and is seen in the form of a large number of rock paintings throughout the park. The age of the paintings is not easy to determine, but it is possible that some could be over 20,000 years old. If so, Kakadu is the site of some of the most ancient art surviving, and this as much as scenery and wildlife has led to Kakadu's place on the World Heritage List. In this Kakadu is unusual because most items on the List are either cultural entities or natural areas; Kakadu is both.

Some of the best-known art sites are at Ubirr, formerly known as Obiri Rock, and Nourlangie Rock. Ubirr is a large rock formation near the East Alligator River and its main gallery is the site of dozens of paintings. Subjects range from catfish and barramundi to a figure of a white man standing with hands on hips, and even an intriguing depiction of a Tasmanian Tiger, proving that the animal was once found in the Top End. Paintings of European equipment such as rifles and axes are also found around the site, while warriors and other

Left Pandanus palms along Jim Jim Creek. **Above** Superb examples of Aboriginal paintings at the rock formation known as Jabiru Dreaming.

subjects are depicted at sites on top of the rock. A one kilometre walking track makes the art sites accessible to visitors, while many people also follow the rough track to the top of Ubirr to see the views of the lush surrounding countryside and watch the sunset. Free tours are conducted by Park Rangers.

Further south, Nourlangie Rock also features an outstanding range of paintings which are made accessible by well graded walking tracks. Aboriginal Dreamtime figures are prominent, in addition to tribal scenes. Contrary to popular opinion, art sites are usually not sacred sites because they were usually occupation areas used by the whole community, whereas sacred sites could only be visited by men.

South-west of Nourlangie Rock, past the Anbangbang Billabong, are found the Blue Paintings, so called because they are unusual in utilising that colour. Aboriginal painting normally was done with ochres and the predominant colours were black, white and orange. The Blue Paintings were done in the 1950s by an artist known as Barramundi Charlie, who used Reckitts Instant Blue for his blue pigmentation. Barramundi Charlie returned to touch the paintings up in the 1960s, so they were virtually the last paintings done in the park. The Aboriginal artistic tradition lives on and is gaining international recognition, but nowadays the paintings are mostly done on bark. Other blue paintings have been done in Arnhem Land, where blueberries provided the pigmentation.

The area in which the Blue Paintings are situated is rich in sacred sites which are, of course, strictly off-limits to visitors. Quite recently the area has been opened up to visitors on the condition that a Park Ranger must be present to supervise proceedings.

Aboriginal paintings in Kakadu are constantly threatened by deterioration due to exposure to rainwater, and the presence of wasp nests, which can cause extensive damage. A constant battle is fought to protect the paintings from the elements and ensure their survival for as long as possible.

In addition to the ancient tradition of Aboriginal art, some more modern developments have taken place in recent years. Visitors can choose from a wide range of accommodation, from camping grounds like Mel and Mardukal to the more luxurious hotel accommodation at Kakadu Holiday Village and Cooinda Hotel/Motel. The former is situated close to the South Alligator River and provides a camping ground in addition to the motel units. A swimming pool is found nearby and boat rides on the river are a daily occurrence. Swimming in the river is not recommended, however, because the South Alligator, like all Kakadu waterways, is infested with Saltwater Crocodiles. These are affectionately known as "salties" but visitors usually feel more affectionate at a respectful distance. The crocodiles are sometimes seen sunning themselves on the banks of the river.

Cooinda is situated near the Yellow Water Lagoon, a feature of Jim Jim Creek. Boat rides are available on Yellow Water and crocodiles are often sighted. For those who like to stretch their legs, a walking track extends from Cooinda to Yellow Water, an easy walk of a few kilometres that takes in some outstanding wetland scenery.

Some of the most spectacular scenery, however, is found along the Arnhem Land Escarpment, which rambles broadly along the eastern section of the park. Jim Jim Creek tumbles over the escarpment in the wet season, creating the majestic Jim Jim Falls, much loved by photographers but only accessible by helicopter during the Wet. In the Dry season, the area can be reached by four-wheel drive with a walk over rocks along the last kilometre, but unfortunately the falls do not flow at that time of year. About ten kilometres away are the mighty Twin Falls, which can only be reached by swimming upstream from the end of the four-wheel drive track. Most visitors to Kakadu understandably go during the Dry season—winter—but locals will tell you that the best time is the Wet season, when the scenery is green and luxuriant, wildlife abounds and the waterfalls flow.

Katherine Gorge National Park

About a hundred kilometres south of Kakadu is its sister park, Katherine Gorge National Park. The two parks are linked by the Katherine River, which rises in the southern part of Kakadu and flows south to the town of Katherine. The river was named by John McDouall Stuart, after one of the daughters of his patron, James Chambers. Ludwig Leichhardt

Above right The Anbangbang Billabong near Nourlangie Rock. **Following pages** Tourists walk along the top of Obiri Rock.

had been the first European explorer to enter the area, doing so in 1844. A town later developed along the banks of the river, near the old ford now known as Knotts Crossing. The town on the river became a welcome stop for travellers making the long, hot journey north, all the more so since the Katherine River was the first permanent running water encountered on the way. The area was immortalised by Aeneas Gunn in her novel "We of the Never Never", and is now a thriving centre.

Thirty kilometres from the town is Katherine Gorge, the centrepiece of a national park that encompasses over 180,000 hectares of land. The park has become one of the most popular tourist attractions in the Northern Territory, with its combination of rugged cliffs, river scenery, escarpment walking tracks and Aboriginal paintings. In the western part of the park visitors can also find Edith Falls, one of the least known attractions of the park. The area features, in addition to the falls themselves, a waterhole surrounded by monsoon forest, while more energetic visitors can walk over the escarpment to the pools and rapids above the falls.

Escarpment walks are also a feature of the main gorge, where walking tracks start at the visitors' centre and proceed along the escarpment, running parallel to the river. A number of off-shoots go to various places of interest, including Butterfly Gorge, named after the butterflies that can be seen in profusion on the walls of the gorge. Those who do not wish to walk can go on the popular boat-rides down the river or hire canoes and go as far as they like under their own steam.

Several kilometres downstream there are quite a few Aboriginal paintings. The Katherine area was traditionally the home of the Dagoman and Jawoyn tribes, who left a legacy of paintings throughout the area.

Visitors to Katherine can take advantage of the accommodation in the town or stay overnight at the Katherine Gorge Camp Ground, where they are often intrigued by the hordes of wallabies that are a regular sight in the area. At night, in particular, the wallabies come out to graze on the grass in the camp ground, and provide visitors with a unique experience that puts a finishing touch to their visit to Katherine Gorge.

Above left The steep walls of Katherine Gorge. **Below left** The East Alligator River at sunrise. The river forms a natural divide between Kakadu and Arnhem Land. **Above** Butterfly Gorge, named for the butterflies found on its walls.

Left above Sunset over Obiri Rock, Kakadu.
Left below Yellow Waters billabong, Kakadu.

Above Water buffaloes, now prolific in the Northern Territory, are proving to be a hazard for native flora and fauna.
Right Brown snake, East Alligator River, Kakadu.

A boab tree near the mouth of Katherine Gorge.